FOREX MADE EASY

STEPHEN BENJAMIN

LEGAL NOTICES

COPYRIGHT

All rights reserved. No part of this book may be reproduced in any form whatsoever, electronic or mechanical, including photocopying, recording, or by any informational storage or retrieval system or re-distributed without the express written permission of the author. This book cannot be sold under any circumstance; you have only personal rights to this book.

DISCLAIMER

By using the information in this book you agree that this is general education material and you will not hold anybody responsible for loss or damages resulting from the content provided here by the author

Please note that Forex trading and trading in other leveraged products involves a significant level of risk and is not suitable for all investors. Before undertaking any such transactions you should ensure that you fully understand the risks involved and seek independent advice if necessary. Any opinions, or other information contained in this book are provided for general educative purpose, and do not constitute investment advice.

Copyright © 2017 Stephen Benjamin

All rights reserved.

ISBN:
ISBN-13: **978- 1985875326**
ISBN-10: **1985875322**

DEDICATION

I dedicate this book to Dr. Theophilus Ayodele and Pastor Peter Adeyemi whose financial assistance helped me to realize my dream of becoming a trader. These are my destiny helpers. And to all struggling and losing traders all over the world, who at the verge of giving up decided to give my strategy a try.

TABLE OF CONTENTS

LEGAL NOTICES

DEDICATION

TABLE OF CONTENTS

ACKNOWLEDGEMENT

INTRODUCTION

CHAPTER ONE

    INTRODUCTION TO FOREX TRADING

    UNDERSTANDING YOUR MT4 PLATFORM

    CURRENCY PAIRS

    TYPES OF CHART

CHAPTER TWO

    TREND ANALYSIS

    HOW TO DETERMINE TREND ON THE CHART

CHAPTER THREE

    TRADING WITH KEY LEVELS

    SUPPORT & RESISTANCE- USE OF TRENDLINE

    HOW TO DRAW TRENDLINE SUPPORT/RESISTANCE

CHAPTER FOUR

    TRADING SIGNALS

CHAPTER FIVE

    WHEN A TRADE SETUP WILL FAIL

    SAMPLE IDEAL TRADE SET UP

CHAPTER SIX

    RISK AND MONEY MANAGEMENT STRATEGY

CHAPTER SEVEN
TRADING AS A BUSINESS 72
CHAPTER EIGHT
CONCLUSION 75

ACKNOWLEDGEMENT

In my journey to become a trader, I can't help but be grateful to God who helped me to succeed in this Forex business and all the people He has brought my way who helped me all along to be what I am today. I am lucky to be surrounded by a family who supports me, friends that stood in those hard days, and everyone who has spur me on to success today. I am a better trader and person today, and I can't help but think that you all have a little something to do with that.

To the love of my life, Grace, who believes in me and my future even when there was nothing to show for it. Thanks for believing in me and standing strong and tall by my side. There isn't a day you don't make me feel loved.

To my brother, Theophilus, I owe a great deal of gratitude to you. Your financial gift helped me to kick start my trading journey when I started with stocks back in 2012. I don't know what I ever did to deserve this, but it must have been grand. You are my hero, and the best reason I am what I am today.

To my Life Mentor Peter Adewole, he is always ready to assist me to become the best God want me to be. Your loan to learn Forex and Invest has brought me here. I am grateful you are always there when I need you. Thank you.

To my Forex Mentor Mr Segun Ajayi, I owe deep sense of gratitude for putting me through step by step on how to trade. We not only became forex buddy but more than friends. Thank you for taking the time to replicate yourself in me.

And finally to everyone who didn't believe Forex works and saw me as wasting my time and effort when I keep losing and nothing seems to work. You are the very reasons I didn't give up and breakthrough in Forex. I appreciate you all.

INTRODUCTION

Forex Trading is one of the easiest businesses a man can set up. It does not require much start-up capital like you would if you are to establish a physical business. With a good device like a laptop or tablet, internet connection and a good broker, you can start with as low as $100.

You may ask if Forex is that easy, why is everyone not making it in Forex? People who have been into it and lost several thousands of dollars will discourage you not to waste your time venturing into the business saying is a scam. It is better to set up a physical business you can see and control than watching one chart and waiting to see your money vanish in a twinkle of an hour. If you talk about investing into Forex business, they see you as a gambler who has no work.

The truth is Forex works and is one of the easiest means to make money online only if you have a **trading edge**. If you ask most people who lost money what did you trade? Why did you trade this set up? They will not be able to clearly define their trading edge and what they see before placing their trade.

To succeed in Forex trading, you need to acquire the right skills, developed your confidence through demo trading and knows the right trading strategy that suits your personality.

Forex is not about pulling the trigger when you see a big move; you need to have a **TRADING EDGE**. A Trading edge is what defines if you will succeed in this business or not. Your trading edge is the signals you are looking for in the market that will inform you when to buy and when to sell.

This book is written to fill the gap by giving you the right trading edge that will help you to trade profitably in the market. If you have been trading before and you barely break even, or you are a beginner in the Forex business, I strongly believe implementing the strategies as explained in the chapters of the book will help you to realize your dream of making a success of Forex business. This trading edge works in all market and in all time frames.

I implore you to follow me as I teach you step by step how you can trade profitably without much knowledge of advance Forex techniques and still make money from the Forex market.

You don't need much knowledge of advance techniques to trade profitably. Simplicity is the key. Keep it simple and you will be among the few profitable traders out there living on Forex trading. This book is written to help you become a successful trader.

Trading is fun and interesting. Follow me as I open to you what you need to do to succeed. I hope you will find this book useful and helpful in your trading journey.

Stephen

FOREX MADE EASY

CHAPTER ONE

INTRODUCTION TO FOREX TRADING

I want to work with the understanding that you are not new to the basis of Forex Trading. With this understanding, I will go straight to treat the main course in details.

One of the first things I will let you know as a trader (whether you are beginning or struggling or losing) is that if you want to trade successfully. Start with the **DAILY CHART** or **DAILY TIMEFRAME**. Do you hear that? Daily time frame. That is your first secret to making it as a Forex trader. Oh! I hear you say, do you mean people trading 1hr, 5mins, 30mins, 4hrs don't trade profitably? No! Not at all. What am suggesting to you is that, if you are still losing money and finding it difficult to make sustainable profit in Forex market. Your number one enemy you must fight is any time frame below the daily time frame. The truth is you need enough experience, concentration and fast decision making to trade a lower time frame. And this is one of the reasons you may be losing so much money.

As a matter of fact, do your research very well, most brokers will not advise you to trade the daily chart because they know you will make fewer mistakes and you will profit more. You tend to lose more in the lower time frame than you do in daily and this is to their advantage. And besides, may I tell you that most professionals' traders don't trade any timeframe less than the daily chart. At best, they can still trade the 4hrs timeframe, but anytime frame lower than this; they regard it as noise.

So in a nutshell, if you want to turn your losses to winning, follow my advice. Stop trading the lower time frames and concentrate on the daily chart for now until you gain experience and confidence to trade the lower time frame.

UNDERSTANDING YOUR MT4 PLATFORM

If we are on the same page now, then I will like to use this space to talk more about the MT4 platform. If you already know how to use it, you can skip this page. But for new or beginning traders this will be good for them.

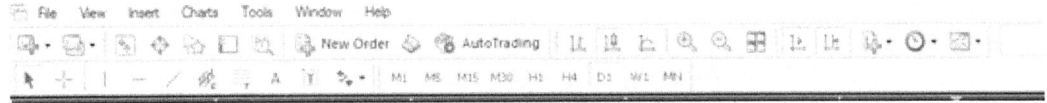

This is typical sample of what you will see on your broker's MT4 platform.

When you want to buy or sell, you will click on NEW ORDER as shown below

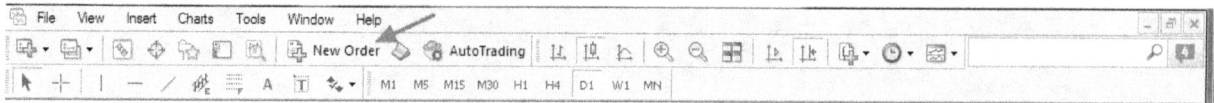

It will bring up a page as shown below

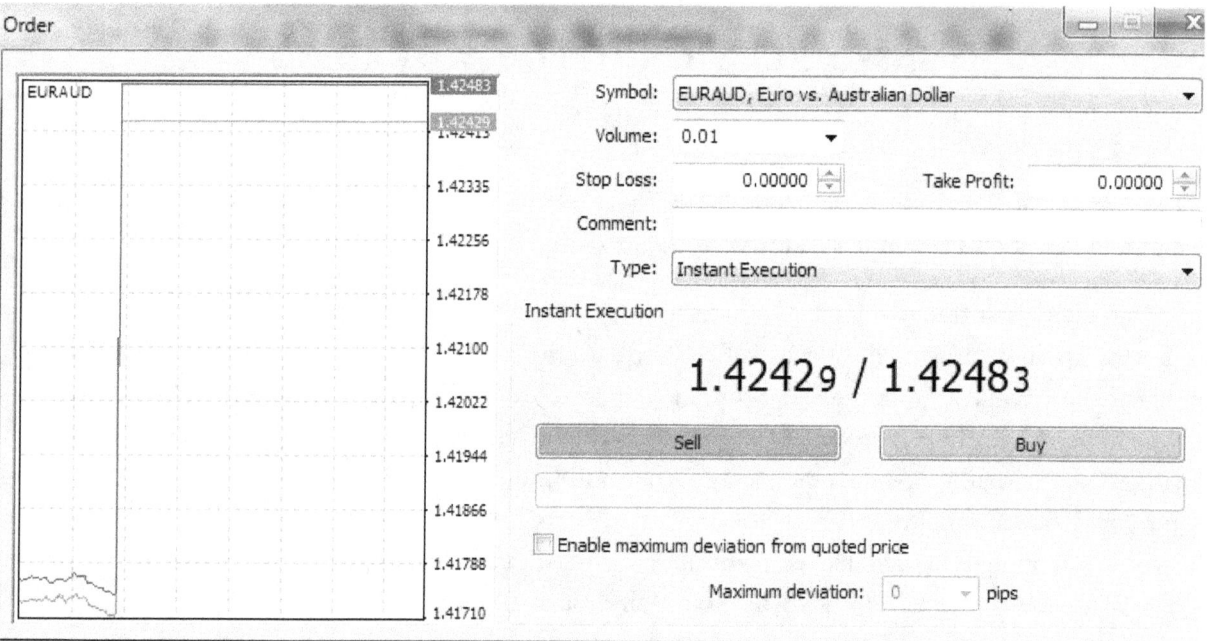

You can see **Symbol** that is the currency pairs you are trading. In this case it is EURAUD or Euro Vs Australian Dollar; it could be GBPUSD, EURUSD, and USDJPY depending on the currency pair you want to trade.

The next Item is **Volume.** Volume is the lot size you want to trade. Is like saying, quantity of trade you want the broker to open for you. The Smallest is 0.01 volume, You can see 0.01 till 8.00 lot size. The Volume you trade with will determine the value of the pip giving to you in dollars when you make profit or lose. If you choose 1.00 lot, your pip value will be $10 or approximately $10 depending on the currency pair. 0.01 lot will give you $0.1 pip, 0.02lot will give you $0.2 in value. 2 lot will give you $20 etc. You can open a demo account to know the equivalent for each lot size in dollar because the values differs depending on the type of account you open-mini, micro or standard account.

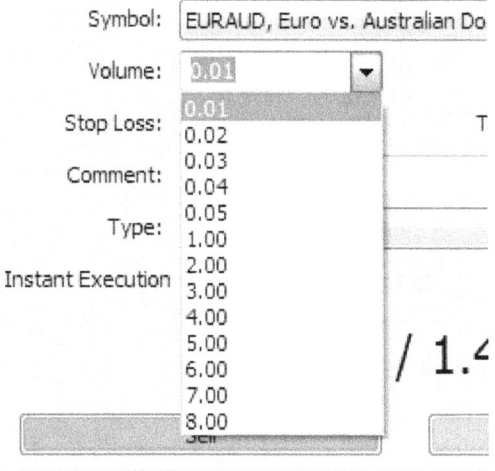

STOP-LOSS

This is the order given to your broker to take you out of the market in case the trade fails and goes against you. In such a case, you are telling your broker that if this trade reverses against my analyze direction, take me out of the market at this level to stop my loss.

NOTE: It is very important you input stop loss in trading, or else you are inviting tsunami. Imagine this scenario in the GBPCHF chart below, imagine you are buying this trade and you didn't put stop loss, your account will be blown by such unforeseen occurrences like this. So STOP LOSS is a MUST.

TAKE PROFIT

This is the price level you set in such a way that if price move in your favor and price reach that level, the broker should take your profit and add it to your account balance. Or an order in term of price given to your broker to take your profit once the price moves to your target price level.

TYPE

The order to buy or sell can be Instant as shown above or a pending order. Instant order is when you buy at the current market price. If at the moment in the market the price for EURUSD is 1.4200/1.4203 To Order at market price or Instant Order is to buy or sell at this price without waiting for the price to come down or go up before you take action.

PENDING ORDER: Pending Order is into 4 categories.

BUY LIMIT

This is to buy below the current market price. This happen when you forsee that the price will come down (retrace) and instead of buy at a high price, let me buy when the price is cheaper than what the market offering me now. In this case, you place a buy limit.

SELL LIMIT

This is to sell the market when you have done your analysis and forsee that the market will likely go up before it finally sell (retrace). This is an order used to short the market. If the price currently is 1.201 and you see that it will get to 1.220 and hit a resistance (a level it cannot push up again before coming down) then you place a sell limit at 1.220. In that case once the market gets there, the broker will place a sell trade for you.

BUY STOP

Is an order given to your broker to buy the market when the price is above the current market price. Assuming you want to trade buy on EURUSD. And you forsee that it might likely sell before it buys and you are not sure or you see a resistance which might likely cause the price to retrace or fall. In such a case, we place buy Stop to join the market once the market has finally able to break the resistance and in order not to miss the opportunity. It is this type of order that help us to join the opportunity.

SELL STOP

Is an order given to your broker to sell the market for you when the price is below the current market price. This is done in a case when you want to be sure the market is actually going in the intended direction before you join the market. Assuming you want to trade sell on EURUSD. And you forsee that it might likely buy before it sells and you are not sure or you see a support which might likely cause the price to retrace or bounce up. In such a case, we place Sell Stop to join the market once the market has finally able to break the support and in order not to miss the opportunity. It is this type of order that help us to join the opportunity.

The next item you see is **Sell and Buy.** And the price at which you sell or buy at the market. If you look at that price you see 1.42429/1.42483. If you are buying EURAUD you buy at 1.42483 and if you are selling you will sell at 1.42429. The difference between these two prices is the spread.

SPREAD

This is the amount charge by broker for each sell or buy you place on their platform on each currency pair. And it is calculated by subtracting the buy from the sell. In case of the above example, the spread is (1.42429-1.42483) which is 0.00054. In real sense, disregard the 0000 before 54. This broker charge 5.4pips for EURAUD pair. Some can charge more or less, it depends on the broker. Spread is how brokers make their money from traders legally.

TIME FRAME

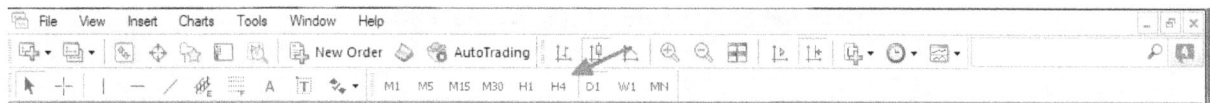

The time frame starts from 1mins, 5mins, 30 mins, 1hr, 4hrs, daily, weekly and monthly time frame. The red arrow shows where you can find it on the MT4

INDICATORS

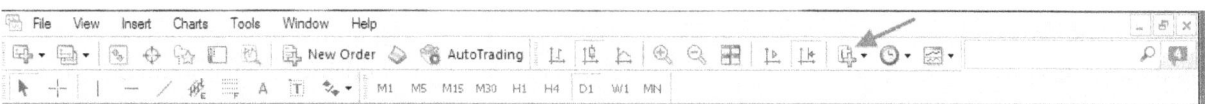

This Green Icon is where you can insert Indicators to add to your chart. See list of Indicators below

FOREX MADE EASY

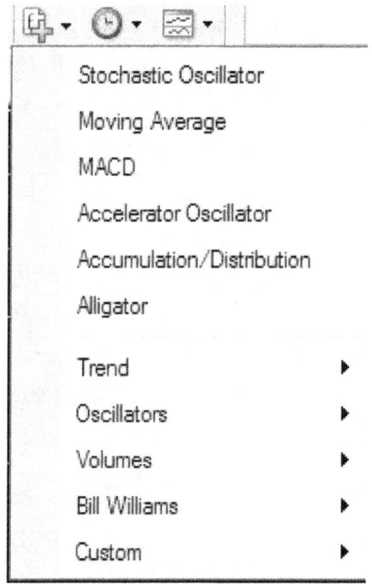

ZOOM IN/OUT

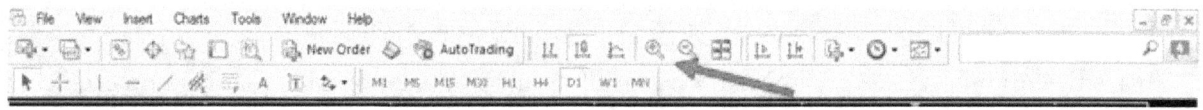

This is what you will press to zoom in or zoom out your chart. That is, to reduce the size of the chart or enlarge the chart.

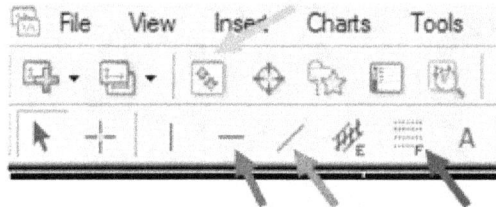

Blue Arrow-It indicates Horizontal line. Whenever you want to draw support and resistance, you click on it to draw horizontal line for support and resistance.

Green Arrow- It indicates Trendline. Trendline is also use to draw support and resistance. You click on that arrow when you want to draw Trendline.

Purple Arrow: It indicates Fibonacci. Fibonacci is also one of the trading tools you can use for trading. But in this manual, you may not necessary need it or use it.

Yellow Arrow: It indicates the market watch. It is here you can see all the currency pairs and commodities to trade. See picture below. You can see Bid/Ask is same as Sell/Buy

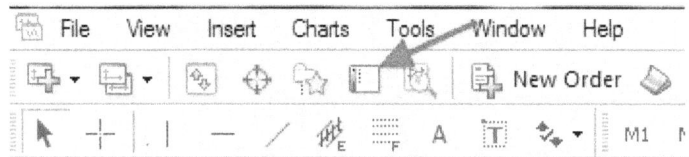

Then you click on this icon as shown in the picture below

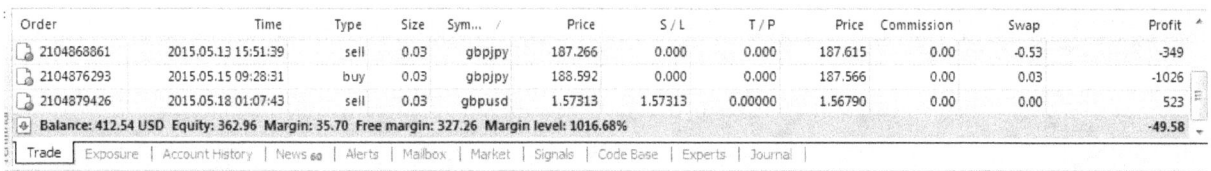

You will see this as shown in the snap shot below

EQUITY

This is your capital. Assuming you deposit $100 today into your trading account. That $100 is your equity. And the more profit you gain through trading, it will be added to your equity, likewise if you lose, it will be debited from your equity.

BALANCE

Balance is your equity +/- your profit or loss. For instance, in the above snap shot, the balance is $412; the equity is $362.96 while the profit is -$49.58. This means, assuming there is no negative profit of -$49.58, the potential total amount of money is $412. If the trade is successfully close in profit, that profit will be added to the equity and it will be the total balance in your account.

MARGIN

Margin is the amount of money your broker will take from your equity/capital to open a trade for you anytime you requested to buy or sell. It is like this. You want to buy goods from Walmart stores to resell. The money you take to Walmart to trade is refer to as margin in forex trading. Assuming I am opening a buy on EURUSD, the broker will take about $24 from my account to open that trade. If the trade is successful, and I close my trade in profit, the margin together with the profit will be added back to my account.

FREE MARGIN

Free margin is the amount or balance remaining from your equity when your broker has already open a trade for you. Or we can say the money left in your account which is yet to be traded.

CURRENCY PAIRS

In Forex trading, the major currency pairs are EURUSD- the most traded currency in Forex market, GBPUSD, USDJPY, USDCHF, USDCAD, AUDUSD, NZDUSD. We also have cross currency pairs like GBPNZD, GBPAUD, EURAUD, GBPCAD, AUDJPY, AUDCHF etc.

We also trade commodities like Gold, Silver, Oil, Gas etc.

I believe you are familiar with all these. Now you may ask, which pair should I trade? Every pair is tradable. We trade the ones that give us the signal we are looking for.

I trade all pairs at least majority about 20+ together with Gold and Oil.

TYPES OF CHART

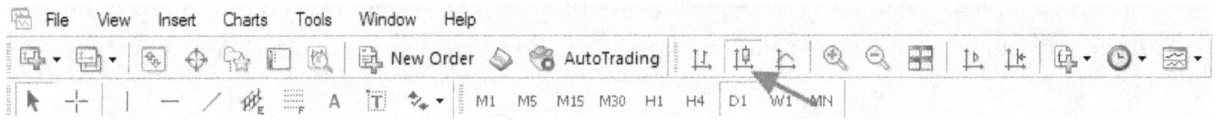

On the MT4 platform when you click on the icon indicated by the RED arrow, the first one is **bar chart,** the middle icon is **candlesticks** and the last icon is **line chart.**

For proper and best analysis, we use candlestick chart. Before the introduction of candlesticks by the Japanese, bar chart was mostly used in the western world. Now we prefer candlesticks chart better because it helps us to analyze the sentiment of market participants better than bar chart and line chart.

Let see what a typical candlesticks depicts.

In the snap shot below you see what a typical candlestick looks like

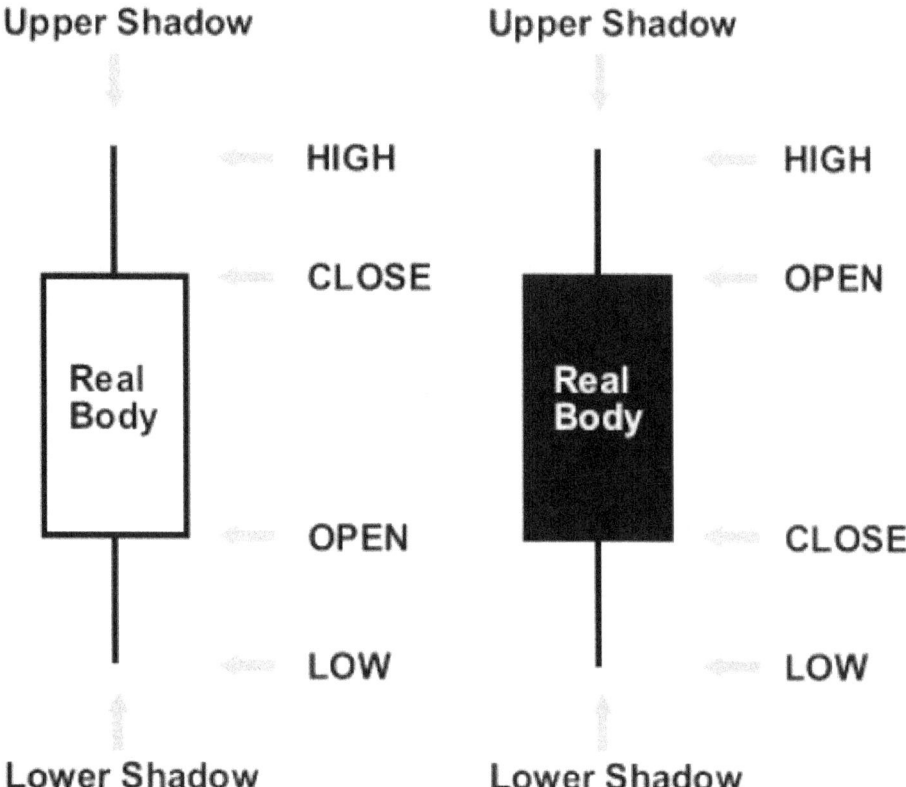

Open- This is the price at which the market first of all traded when the market opens or start.

Low- This is lowest price that the market got to during that trading period.

High- This is the highest price that the markets got to or traded during a given period of time.

Close- This is the price at which the market stop trading during a given period of time.

For instance, assuming on 18th Jan 2015, when the market opens EURUSD open price was 1.1200, traders started trading until the price drops to 1.1000 for that day. All of a sudden, there was a huge buying that drove the price up to 1.1300 and by the time the market will close the price closed with 1.1289. Now the Open price is 1.1200, the Low Price is 1.1000; the high is 1.1300 while the close price is 1.1289.

The Lowest price for a given time period can also be shown with a lower shadow while the highest price will be indicated by the Upper shadow.

This is depicted with a candlestick in a similar fashion as shown above in the snapshot.

FOREX MADE EASY

A TYPICAL CANDLESTICKS CHART

BULLISH CANDLE

When the Price close above the opening price for a given time period (it could be 1min, 5min, 15mins 1hr, a day etc), the candle is bullish. In such a case, there is a buy or a rally. It also means that buyers outnumber or overpower the sellers and they drove price up from where it opens to the close of that time period. The green arrow shows a bullish candle where the price at close is above the price at open. Or the closing price is greater than the open price.

BEARISH CANDLE

When the price close below the opening price for a given time period, we have a bearish candle. It is indicated by the red arrow. Bearish candle always indicate that the selling pressure was greater than the buying pressure for a given time period. Sellers outnumber the buyers and price fell.

CHAPTER TWO

TREND ANALYSIS

The Second thing you must do to trade profitably is

- ➢ Know the Trend for the Pair you want to Trade and;
- ➢ Trade with the Trend.

It is a commonly known slogan in Forex that the trend is your friend. Yes it is! Trading against the trend will cost you your capital. You are inviting failure if you break this rule.

What is the Trend?

The Trend is the direction of the market. Where the market is heading to. Trend could be Up or Down or Sideways. That is, is the market going up or down or moving sideways.

These are the three basic types of market direction we can have.

- ✓ UP TREND
- ✓ DOWN TREND
- ✓ SIDEWAYS/RANGING/CONSOLIDATING MARKET.

UP TREND

You are going to determine an Up Trend when the market or price is having higher highs and higher lows. For instance look at the chart below (GBPJPY Daily Chart)

You can see from the chart that price is increasingly moving higher. In such a case the trend is UP. Let's see another example. GBPZND Daily Chart

In such a case, we see that the price keep having higher highs, and higher lows. So the Trend is UP. Let's see another example. This is CADJPY daily chart

Price is in an UP trend on this Pair.

DOWN TREND

We determine a down trend when price keep making lower highs and lower lows. Remember when the price continues to make lower highs and lower lows, the trend is down. But when price keep making higher highs and higher lows, the trend is UP.

For instance, look at this EURUSD pair.

You can see that price is in a down trend for a long period of time. Every attempt to rally or go up was nullify by several move down. Price keeps making lower highs and lower lows for a long period of time.

Let see another example. AUDUSD Daily chart

You can see that price move from the top @ 0.88620 to as low as 0.76545 before trying to go up. This is a down trend.

SIDEWAYS/RANGING MARKET

When price is neither moving up nor moving down but seem to be contained within a price range. Such a market is ranging. It can also be referred to as a consolidating market. Let take a look at USDJPY chart for instance

If you observe you can see that the price ranges between 118.365 and 120.890 for quite some time before it tried to break the upper horizontal line upward.

This is another example of a ranging market. AUDCAD daily chart.

HOW TO DETERMINE TREND ON THE CHART

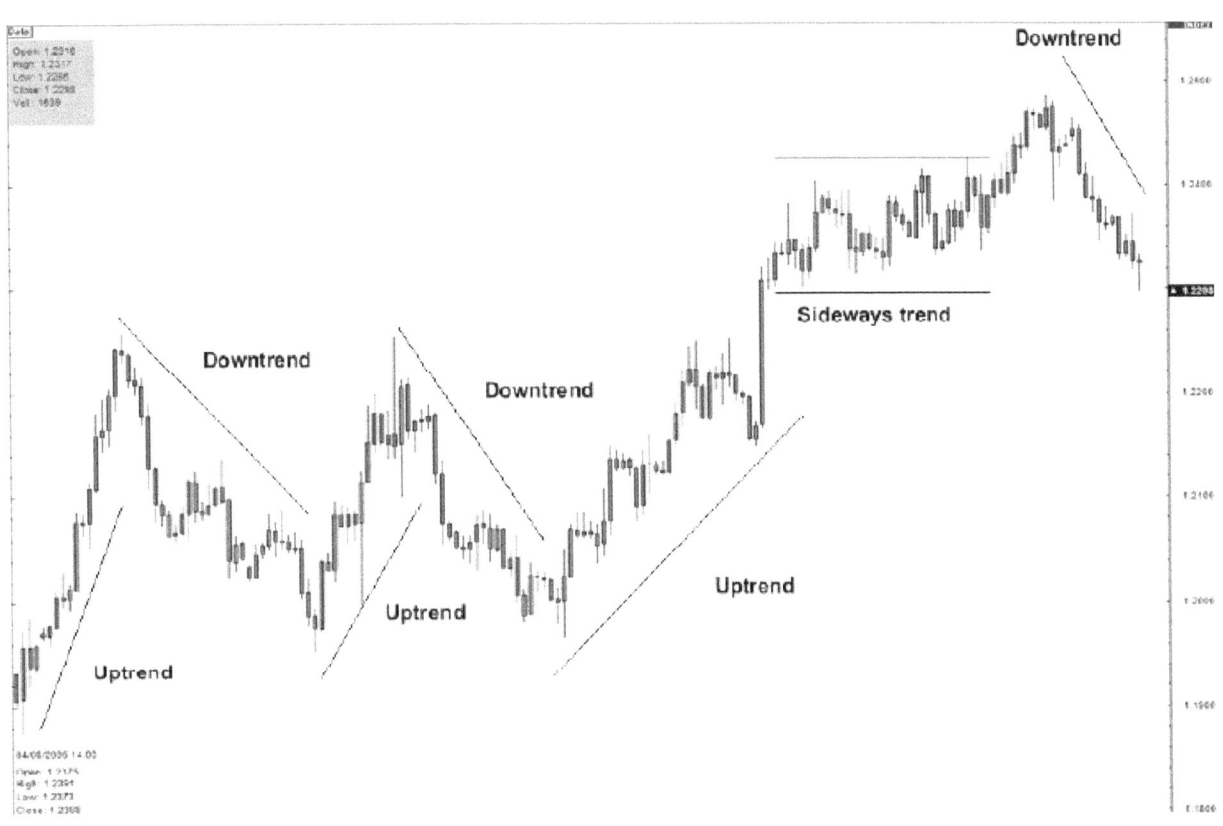

Now that you know how to determine the trend. What do you do next?

"Trade in Line with the Trend - That is if the trend is UP, you are going to trade any buy signal. And if the trend is Down you are going to trade Sell Signal"

This is very important.

If you trade against the trend of the market, the probability of losing money is 95% high than losing when you are trading with the trend.

It is just like swimming with the tide of the sea. Even an inexperience swimmer will swimmer successfully than when you are swimming against the tide.

Trend is a key important aspect of trading.

CHAPTER THREE

TRADING WITH KEY LEVELS

The third important key thing you must do is to determine the Key Levels on the chart. Remember we are dealing with the daily chart. So you must draw your

- ✓ Resistance and;
- ✓ Support levels

What are Key Levels?

They are the zones on the chart at which the movement of the price was stalled. A currency pair that is moving up strongly will get to a point that the movement will be halted and it start falling before it resumes the upward movement. Likewise a falling pair will get to a point where the price will temporarily cease to fall and rise for some time before it continues its downward movement.

For instance, if you throw a ball into the air, no matter how fast it moves up, when it get to a time, the force of gravity will acts on it until the pace decrease and after some time, it will hit a point in the air that the ball will bounce back and start falling. That point at which the ball reverses its direction is a key zone.

The two most important Key zones on the chart are Resistance and Support Level.

However, please note that these are not horizontal lines drawn on the chart, is more of a zone than a line.

- **Resistance-** When price is in an uptrend- going up. The level or Zone at which this up trend pause to start falling is call Resistance. In such a case, the price has hit a level that the momentum of the price at the moment was unable to break, hence a change of direction for some time.
- **Support-** When price is falling or in a down trend. The level or zone at which a falling price get to and stop falling to change is direction to upward movement is call Support.

These two are the 2 key levels that must be determined on a chart after you have determined the trend of the market. For instance, look at this CADCHF chart.

CHART ANALYSIS

You can see that the price journey from the bottom on 19th Jan 2015 move up strongly until it hit a point it couldn't continue that upward journey. It hits Resistance at Arrow 2, unable to break it upward, it reverses direction until it gets to a point around Arrow 3 where the fell, was held or supported. You can see that from March 26th to April 3rd, price was dancing around this level, unable to break it downward to continue its bearish journey. It rose to test the previous height again hoping if it can break it, but the level prove too strong for it to break and return again to test the support to see if it can be broken too. But these two levels seem to held price and it moves up and down in between these zones.

The point or zone at which Price movement is curtailed is the key zone as you can see in the chart above. Once you check the chart and you can spot this, all you have to do is draw a horizontal line to demarcate this on the chart.

You may have to look far behind, i.e you can check as far as 2 -3 months ago on the daily chart or weekly chart to know where there is sharp change in price movement on the chart.

It is important to do this because; it will guide you to know the caution zones or danger zone while you trade. If an area or zone has been a resistance or support in the past, when price gets to this zone again, the price will like to respect the zone.

As a matter of fact, most traders see the zone as you are seeing it too, so those that are already in profit will like to take off their profit from the market and this will cause price to respect the zone or pause its movement a bit except in case of any major economic news that gave momentum to price to break that barrier.

Let's see another example, NZDJPY daily chart

You can see that in all the places where you see those horizontal arrows, there was a reaction of price to those levels. When price gets to those zones, it pauses and changes direction.

Drawing your Key Zones like this make the chart more easier to analyze than leaving it blank like below.

You can see that the previous chart is easier to analyze than this one above because you have drawn the Resistance and Support level.

Please also note that like I have said before, these are not just lines, they are more of Zones than lines. For instance take a look at the same chart below

FOREX MADE EASY

RED ARROW

You can see that the first time price reach the upper border of the blue rectangle @ 91.879 on 23rd March 2015, while the 2nd time it tested the same level to know whether it will break or not, the price rose past 91.879 to reach 92.366 on 22nd April, 2015 before it fell when the level was unable to hold. The Resistance Zone is from 91.879- 92.366 and price was unable to break this zone.

GREEN ARROW

On 1st April, 2015, price got to $88.730 before it rally. Now the same zone was tested again on 14th April, 2015, price didn't get to the previous low ($88.730) before it reverses its direction. It touched $89.012 then move up. The fact that it didn't reach the previous low before it change direction does not mean, it didn't get to the support level. In that area or zone, support is available and this held the market from further falling.

I hope this point is understood. See the Key level as more of Zones than level. Because price might not get to the exact price level of the previous high or low before it reverses its direction.

WHAT TO DO?

This is how you are going to go about drawing your Support and Resistance. Take for instance the GBPUSD Daily chart below.

> Once you open you desire chart

- Then Zoom out the chart to have a wider view of the chart- both past and present as you can see below
- Then look for areas on the chart where price has been rejected in its movement either up or down
- Mark those areas with horizontal lines
- When you do this, the chart will be more meaningful to you, it will aid analysis and you will know ahead of time, likely areas to take your profit or to enter the market to trade.

N.B Support and Resistance area helps you to know when to enter the market to trade and where to exit the market to book your profit.

It should interest you to know that you **BUY @ SUPPORT while you SELL @ RESISTANCE**

Let see a typical example GBPUSD Daily Chart

The black horizontal line marks the resistance level where the arrows are.

1st RED Arrow

On 27th Nov, 2014, price rose as high as 1.58245, the rally was not sustained and fell. On 16th Dec. 2015 there was a 2nd attempt to break that level.

2nd RED Arrow

Price retests the level and fell again. This will give you clue that the level is strong. Now once you determine this. Watch for what price will do next time it touches the level again. You can see that in the distance future, 14th May, 2015 price touched that same resistance zone again and unable to break it upward close bearish on 15th March, 2015 and fell drastically.

The fact that you have already marked the level by drawing the resistance line before will keep you on the watch to know what price will do on getting to that same level again. Once you see that price couldn't break and close bearish on the following day, you will now place a Sell trade, depending on the nature of the candlestick pattern you see around that level.

SUPPORT & RESISTANCE- USE OF TRENDLINE

Trend line is also another tool in trading to mark support and resistance level on the chart. It also gives us a clue to where there might likely be support and resistance in the nearest future. So it projects likely area on the chart where price might meet with resistance or support.

The green arrow below shows how to locate Trend line on the MT4.

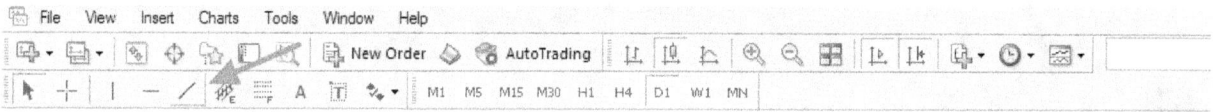

HOW TO DRAW TRENDLINE SUPPORT/RESISTANCE

- ✓ In an uptrend, you will connect 2 lows together with a trend line.
- ✓ While in a downtrend, you will connect 2 highs together with a trend line.

Let's see how to do this. Take for example this GBPAUD Daily chart

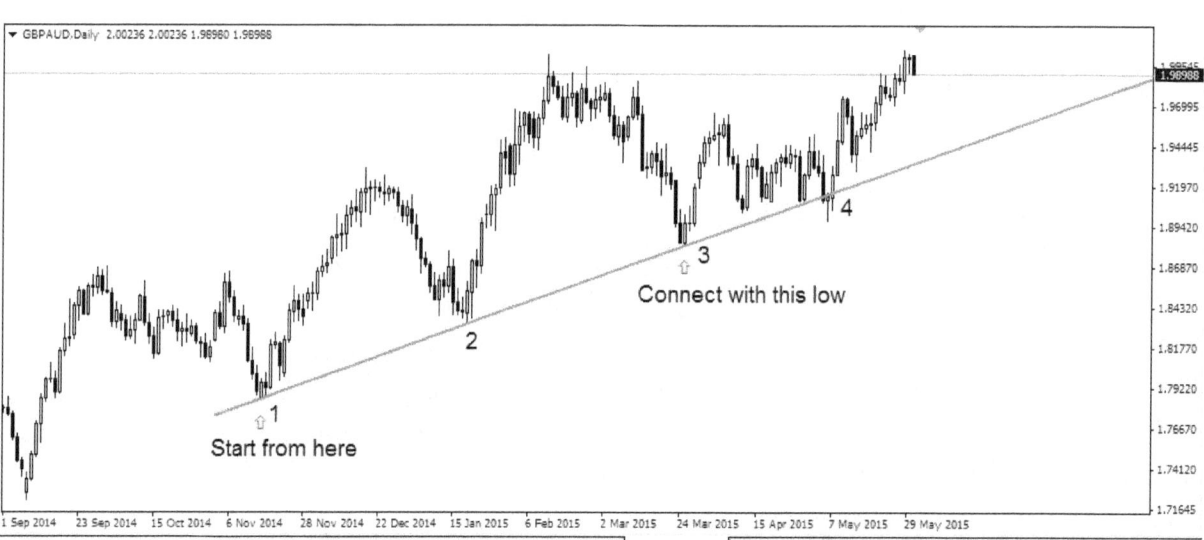

To draw Trend line,

You will connect two lows together if the trend is bullish. As you can see above, we connect the low @ point 1 with the low @ point 2. Now assume price is still at the point 2 when you connect the 2 lows together.

On 25th March, 2015 Point 3, when price get to the trend line, you can see that price respect the support depicted by the trend line. What it means is that, when price has not reach that place when you plotted it in the past, the trend line is telling you that in the future, when price get to the area, it might likely be supported and held from further falling. That was exactly what happens. The price was supported and price rebound and rally to a new high.

At Point 4, you can see that price came back to test that same trend line support again. It appears to have broken it, only to rally back and move away.

When you draw Trend line like this, it will give you clue on areas where you should take caution when you are trading or areas to place trade.

<u>Trend line on EURUSD Daily chart</u>

I have drawn different possible ways of connecting 2 highs or lows together with a trend line.

However just as Support and Resistance can be broken by price, please also note that Trend line can be broken.

FOREX MADE EASY

Look at the same EURUSD chart, the upper trend line provides resistance, preventing the price from going up. While the lower trend line provides support for the price. The lower trend line was broken by that big strong bearish candle (blue arrow) and price left the range or consolidation to move strongly downward.

Let's do a recap-

- Determine the pair to trade base on the signal you see
- Determine the trend- Trade only in line with the trend
- Mark all the Key Levels- Support and Resistance

CHAPTER FOUR

TRADING SIGNALS

Once you have determined the trend and the Key levels. The next thing you should look for on the chart is the **TRADING SIGNALS.**

Trading Signals are key clues that will tell you the next line of action to take. It helps you to know when to buy and when to sell. Most times traders lose because they don't have an edge in the market. Trading is not just about seeing a big move and enters the market. You must have an edge you are looking for in the market. Once you see the set up, then you are okay to place your trade.

Trading signals are our edge in trading. These are the keys we are looking for on the chart to determine whether to trade now or not. We will be dealing with the candlesticks charts for our analysis. To effectively and successfully trade profitably in the market, these are what you should trade (look for).

These signals are reliable, proven over time and they are consistent in giving you an edge to make money from the market.

- ✓ <u>**Trading Signal One: The Pin Bar**</u>

Pin bar are candlesticks with a very long tail and a short small body at the opposite end close to the nose of the candlesticks. They look like this

You can see a very long tail with a small body close to the other end. It could be a bullish pin bar like this.

Or bearish pin bar like this below

What does Pin bar suggests?

Pin bar suggests rejection of a price level. It means anywhere it is form; market participants are rejecting either the low or high price in that zone. They tell you that the market sentiment has change and they always in most cases reverse the trend of the market. For instance, if a bearish pin bar is form at the top of an uptrend, it will reverse the trend to a down trend. Likewise when you find pin bar at the bottom of the trend, it means traders are rejecting low price and you should look to buy.

Bearish Pin bar suggests SELL while Bullish Pin Bar suggest BUY

Let's see from the chart how Pin bar works.

FOREX MADE EASY

4hrs Chart of Crude Oil

et see another chart: AUDJPY Daily chart

have marked where the pin bar was formed and you can see how the direction changes after

FOREX MADE EASY

Pin Bar on GBPJPY Daily Chart

Pin Bar Trade on GBPJPY Daily Chart

Pin Bar Trade in direction of the Trend

You can see that Pin bar works.

How do you trade Pin Bar? There are 3 ways you can trade Pin Bar.

- ✓ You can enter the market immediately after its formation
- ✓ Wait for a retracement to half of the length of the Pin bar
- ✓ Place a pending order

Let's take a look at how to do it. Assuming we want to trade this Pin bar formed on 14th April, 2015 as shown in the chart below. You must ask yourself some questions to aid your analysis.

- ✓ Is it formed on a Key level? Yes there is a support where it formed (Red Horizontal line)
- ✓ What type of signal is it? Pin bar- Reversal Candlesticks- A rejecting candle

✓ Price has been rejected around that zone twice in the past before this pin bar was formed. Which tell us that the Support is strong- The Green arrows depicted the various times price tried to break that level and how it was unable to break it. Finally on 14th April, it formed a Pin Bar to tell us, there is a strong rejection of this low price at the support.

Once you have determined all these on the chart. Then how do we trade this Pin bar.

Like I have said previously, you can enter the market immediately the pin bar is formed @ market open the next day which is 15th April, 2015 or you wait for a retracement.

What is a Retracement?

A retracement is a movement of price opposite to its initial previous movement before the price resumes its initial previous directional movement. What do I mean? Is a time in which if a price is going up for some time, the movement will pause, and move down for a while before the price resumed again. It is also call **PULL BACK.** There is always a slogan that if you miss a rally, don't join the trend immediately waits for a pull back. Pull back or retracement is when the price move against its initial direction for a while before it resumes its movement.

In order to buy at retracement, this is what you do. Open the 1hr chart the following day

You can either use an indicator like **Stochastic** to determine when to enter or use **Fibonacci.**

If you are using stochastic- set your settings to 5, 3, 3

The **Green Arrow** shows a move down contrary to the previous up move- that is the retracement. And this was completed when the bullish engulfing candle was formed indicated by the **Blue Arrow.**

At that time, the Stochastic has also cross up which signal a buy (Red Arrow).

Already you have a mindset to trade Buy based on the formation of the Pin Bar on the daily chart. Once you see this set up on 1hr chart, then you can conveniently enter your BUY without fear of losing your money.

The 2nd method is to use Fibonacci to determine your entry. Or you combine both together as shown below.

- Draw your Fibonacci from the low to the high- if it is an uptrend. In a down trend, you draw from the high to the low. In this case, it is an uptrend.
- Wait for a bullish candle to form on either 38.2, 50.0 61.8 or 78.6 levels-They are all known as retracement levels. They also depict Support and Resistance.
- Now enter at the close of the Bullish Candle formed on 50.0 level
- Stochastic also shows buy signal by crossing up.

The next Option is to Place a **Pending Buy.** You can place a pending buy above the high price of 4th April Candle (176.603). Which means once price break this high price, then the broker should fill in your order and you will enter the market.

These are the three ways you can trade Pin Bar.

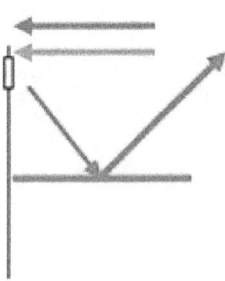

Red Arrow: Enter at Retracement to 38.2, 50.0, 61.8 or 78.6 Fibo Level

Green Arrow: Enter at Market directly without waiting for retracement or break of high

Blue Arrow: Place a Pending Buy above the high of the Pin Bar

- ✓ **Trading Signal Two: Grabber**

Grabber is a form of Pin Bar. It has a long tail but with a bigger body than a pin bar. Grabber is a fake set up pattern. Assuming you place a trade to buy USDJPY @ 120.00 and your stop loss @ 195.00, now instead of the market to buy or move in your direction immediately, it will first of all go against you, hit your stop loss before it reverses direction and move in your intended direction of trade. (i.e. buy) When such happens, it is refer to as a grabber. They are also call Wash and Rinse pattern. They are stop-licking set up. Once you spot such a pattern, they are very powerful price pattern which is accurate in trading.

Grabber could be bearish or a bullish grabber. When grabbers are form, they strongly indicate a major reversal of the trend of a particular swing and the target (take profit) of a grabber is the next available low or high of the swing in which it forms. They are one of the accurate signals I trade. They don't form often, but whenever they come, they are very strong and powerful in changing the mood and direction of the market.

I had once been a victim of grabber trade. I traded against the grabber and I blew away my account. Those are days I was still learning the rope when I don't understand the language of this trading arsenal.

Let me show you some examples of Grabber and how you can place a trader after its formation. Check this EURUSD Daily chart.

The bearish grabber above was formed on 8th May 2014, and since then EURUSD has never recover from the bearish trend caused by the grabber. Can you see below? A powerful bearish trend triggered by the Grabber.

There are numerous example of how grabber works wonder in trading. Please check the follow charts.

FOREX MADE EASY

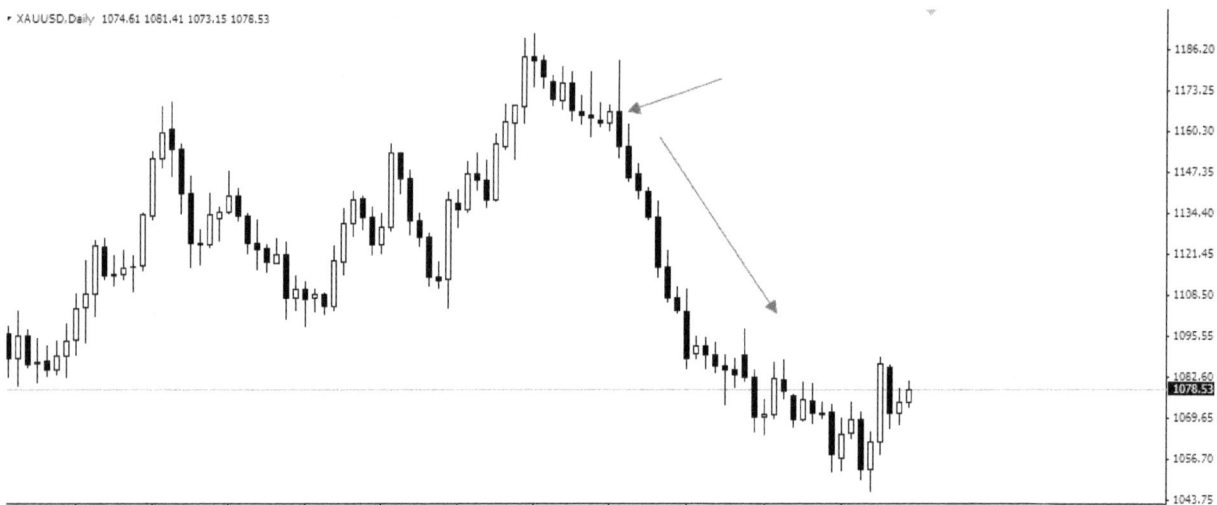

Bearish Grabber on Gold Daily Chart

Crude Oil 4hrs Chart

Crude Oil 1hr Chart

I will like you to scroll back on your chart and look for each of these trading signals and see what happen after their formation. You can back chart to year 2008 and check how many times Pin Bar formed, the number of times it was successful and the failure rate. Likewise do same for grabber. If you check very well, you will find that the failure rate of Pin Bar is about 2 out of 10 trades or even less than that, likewise the grabber. If you trade Pin bar alone, you will surely make consistent money from the market.

You may ask how can I be trading Pin Bar alone and make money? Yes you can be a Pin bar major and make cool consistent money from the market. This is what you will do

- Open so many currency pairs up to 26pairs or 20 pairs as you may like- See mine below

- Draw the key levels
- Then be on the lookout for Pin Bars and Grabbers

I can assure you in a week you will get at least 2 to trade out of all the pairs you open. There are times that you may even get more than 2 or more that you will have to use money management so as not to over trade.

- ✓ **Trading Signal Three: 2 Bar Reversal Pattern**

The 2 bar Reversal pattern is one of the accurate and sweetest price patterns you can trade once the setup is spotted on the chart. It is a **three candlestick price pattern.** The first two candles must trade in the same direction and be a trending candle. The third candle reverses the trend direction by taking out the low of the second candle (for short) or the high of the second candle (for long). (2 Candlesticks has the same color, the 3rd candle has a different color)

This can work either as a Trend Reversal or Trend continuation. We shall look at different examples and see how it works great in line with the trend and as a trend reversal.

This is an example of a 2 Bar Reversal Pattern

GBPCHF Daily Chart

FOREX MADE EASY

GBPNZD Daily Chart

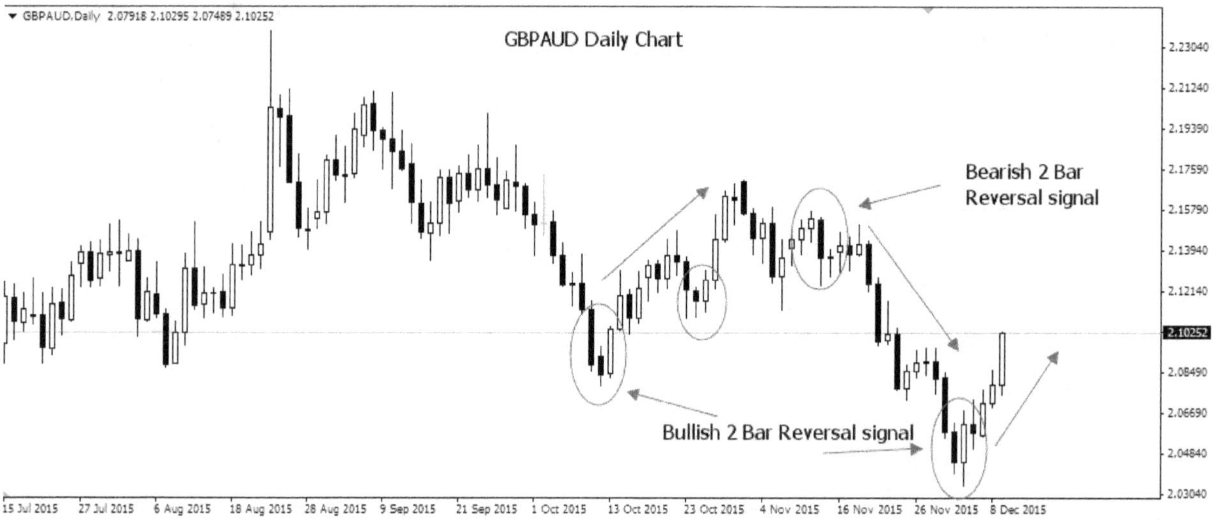

GBPAUD Daily Chart

GBPUSD Daily Chart

GBPUSD Daily Chart

✓ **Trading Signal Four: Engulfing Patterns**

This pattern is a very strong reversal signal at the end of a trend. Engulfing pattern is formed **by two candlesticks with different colors**. The body of the second candlestick should completely engulf the first one. The shadows may also be engulfed but it is not necessary. The first candlestick can also be a Doji. Engulfing pattern is stronger when the first candlestick has a small and the second candlestick has a big body. Also when the second candlestick engulfs more than one candlestick, the pattern is stronger. However, please note that this pattern must be formed on Key levels for it to be a valid trade set up.

If they are formed on support and Resistance, then it will add strength to the signal. If not, you must discard it and look for another set up.

Engulfing patterns could be Bullish Engulfing Patterns or Bearish Engulfing patterns. A **bullish engulfing pattern** is formed at the end of a bearish trend, while a **bearish engulfing pattern** is formed at the top of an Up Trend.

I want to show you several examples of engulfing patterns that formed in different currency pairs and how they were able to reverse the trend of the market.

This is EURAUD Daily chart. I have indicated the Engulfing patterns (both Bearish and Bullish) with the red arrows as shown below

EURAUD Daily Chart

In the chart above, each of the engulfing pattern works as a trend reversal. Secondly you will notice that they are tradable when they are formed on Support and Resistance. I have marked this with the horizontal red line.

EURUSD Daily chart

This is another example of Engulfing Patterns formed on Key levels. The Key Levels are indicated by the red horizontal lines as indicated above in the EURUSD Chart.

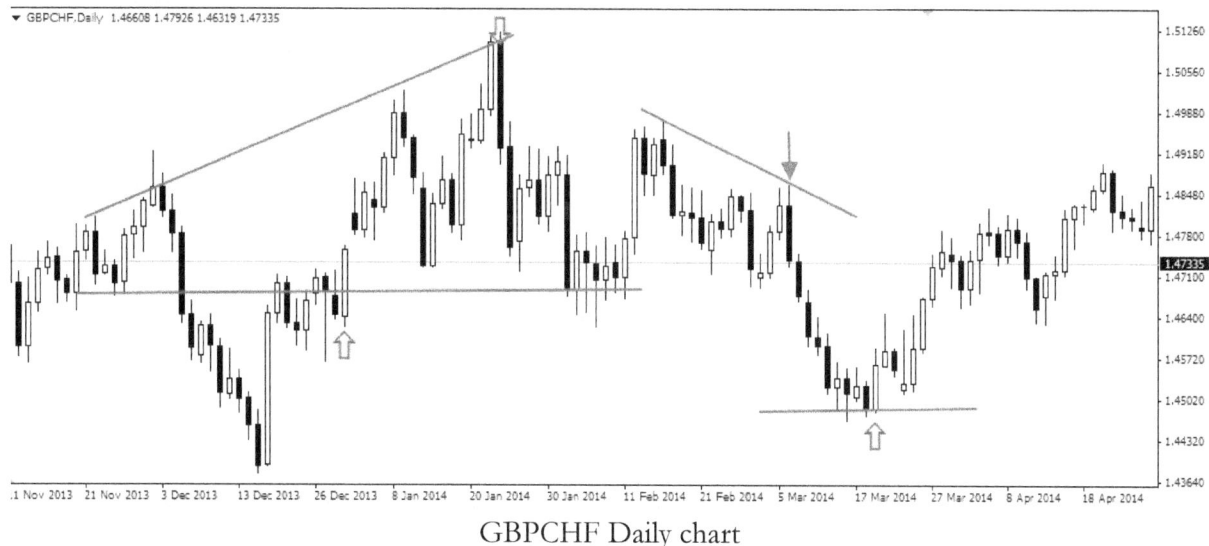

GBPCHF Daily chart

In this GBPCHF pair, I draw the Trendline Resistance and Support and each of the signals was formed around the levels.

This is how to trade any of these signals- whether pin bar, grabber, 2 Bar Reversal or engulfing patterns. Make sure, they are formed on key levels before you ever place your trade.

GBPUSD Daily chart

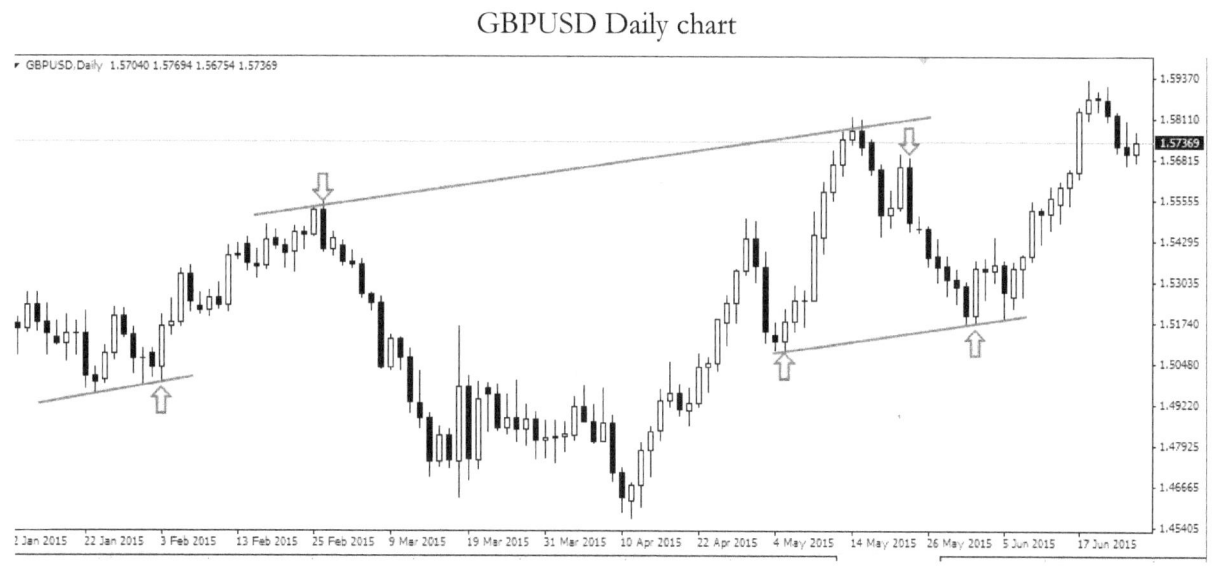

In the chart above, the trendline resistance and support was drawn. And the Engulfing patterns are indicated by the arrows.

USDJPY Daily Chart

Engulfing pattern on EURCAD Daily Chart

From the above chart, price pierce through the support around 1.37540 as marked by the red horizontal line, it was unable to close bearish and reverse upward to engulf the previous 3 trading days.

The next 3 days after was a retracement of the bullish engulfing pattern before price move up to the next resistance at 1.42498

These are few among numerous examples of how engulfing patterns do work as a perfect trading arsenal to beat the market any time any day. This works in all currency pairs even in Commodities and Metals

It is important you develop your confidence in trading these signals. To do this, take your chart and back chart to about 3-4 years ago. Look out for any of these signals. And see what happen after their formation. This will boost your confidence to trade them any time you see them later in the future.

Please note that sometimes, the market may retrace against the set up for some times. It may be a day or 2 days, before the market will now move in the direction of your trade. It happens sometimes, but as long as the low or high of the candle pattern you are trading is not broken, the signal you are trading is still valid.

Once the low or high is broken and the market hit your stop loss, then the trade is invalidated. Count your loss and look forward to another better opportunity nearby. It must be clearly understood that losses are part of the game. It is not bad to lose, provided you didn't lose all your capital at once. That is why you must use good money management to remain in this business.

But with a trading signal like I teach it is impossible to lose consistently if these are what you are trading. I expect that by now, if you have done your home work by back charting, you will discover that the success rate of a Pin Bar is about 8 out of 10 trades. At worst, you win 7 out of 10 trades. This goes with engulfing patterns too. Now if you use controlled money management, even if you lose 5 out of 10 trades, you will still be in profit at the end of the month. We will discuss how to do this later in the next few chapters.

✓ Trading Signal Five: Double Repenetration (DRPO) Pattern

This is a directional pattern trading strategy using a 3x3 moving average. Instead of inputting 3 under period and 0 under Shift, you will use 3x3 as shown below.

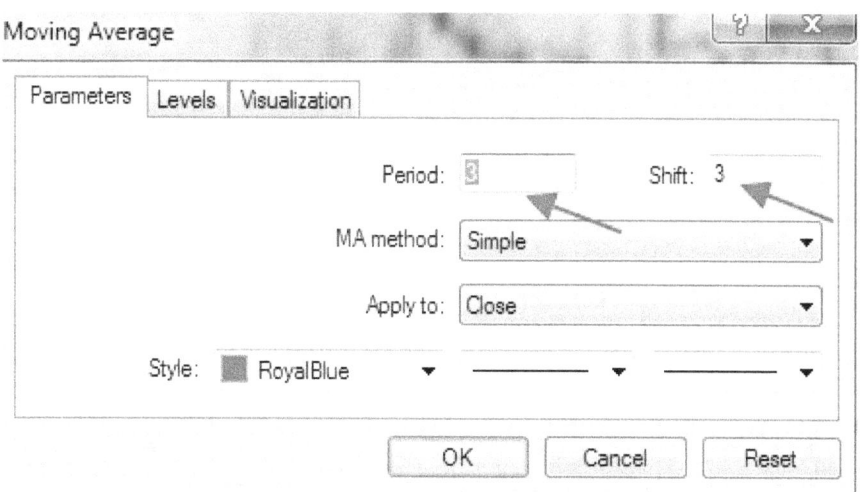

This is how it works. If price is thrusting/trending down, then jumps up across the 3x3 moving average, down again and above again. This is what we can double penetration of displaced moving average. This is a reversal pattern. It indicated the end of a strong trend. This is a zig zag that will often stop many market players out. We have two types DRPO Buy and DRPO sell.

DRPO Buy- When the price is thrusting/trending down, then jumps up across the 3x3 moving average, down again and above again.

DRPO Sell - occurs when the price is thrusting/trending up, then jumps down across the 3x3 moving average, up again and down again.

However please note for this signal to be valid the Double RePo signal candles must be preceded by a minimum of 8-10 periods of thrusting market action (candles); if you get 15 or more is better.

After the up thrust, we need closes below, above, and again below the 3X3, before the sell signal is trigger. The reverse is true for down thrust (buy signal).

Examples of DRPO Trading signal

DRPO Sell on EURUSD Daily Chart

DRPO Sell on Gold 4hrs Chart

DRPO Buy on GBPUSD Daily Chart

The Thrusting/trending market action was down (1) the price jumps up across the 3x3 moving average to (2) then jumps down again to (3) and up again to (4) with a Pin Bar indicating rejection of lower price. The DRPO Buy was confirmed by the Bullish Pin bar and Up the price moves strongly to test the previous high again.

DRPO Sell on EURAUD Daily Chart

This Moving Average also works as Support and Resistance. When price is above the 3x3 moving average, the trend is Up and when the price is below the 3x3 moving average the trend is down. You can also add this understanding to strengthen the signals you are trading.

DRPO Sell on USDCAD Daily Chart

DRPO Sell on EURJPY Daily Chart

✓ <u>**Trading Signal Five: Bread and Butter Trade (B&B)**</u>

It is a directional pattern trading strategy using a 3x3 moving average also. If Price is thrusting/trending down (in a down market), then jumps up across the 3x3 to close for a candle or two candles then continues down to complete the thrusting action.

These look like a pause in the bearish movement of the price and these are often caused by whales-the market movers taking some profit out of a big thrust. They have some positions open to let profits run as the trend continues. The thrust should have at least 8 candles indicating a very strong market sentiment.

. Here's a good example of a Bread and Butter sell. In this daily EUR/USD chart, there is an ascending wedge that breaks at the end of Aug 2011. The thrust is decisive but not 8 perfect down candles. A little jump up but is contained by the 3x3. The market retraces across the 3x3. We get in after the close of the bearish candle because the price action is so decisively down; it is VERY likely to continue down after a little pull ack. It does and continues down. The retracement is usually someone taking profits, not a change in market sentiment.

B&B Sell Trade on EURUSD Daily chart

B&B Sell Trade on EURAUD Daily Chart

B&B Sell Trade on USDCAD Daily Chart

B&B Buy on GBPUSD Daily Chart

After the initial Up thrust, the Price retrace and this retracement was ended with the formation of a bullish engulfing pattern as indicated above. And the price moved strongly upward to test the next resistance level.

You can see in this trade, there many things that strengthen our trade setup. (Conference)
1. We see an engulfing pattern
2. Engulfing pattern with a B&B Buy in the direction of the previous trend.
3. The engulfing pattern was formed around Support Zone.

Whenever you are trading any of these signals, look for conference that will strengthen what you see. What is Conference? These are other factors apart from the signal that will enforce or add strength to the signal you see. We do not trade this signals in isolation. There must be some other key factors that will add value to what we see before we regard the trade as a valid trade set up.

For instance,
➢ What time frame am I looking at? The daily chart time frame is the best.

- What market am I trading? Is it a major Forex pair or a more volatile exotic pair?
- What condition is the market in? Trending, consolidating?
- Where are the obvious key support / resistance levels in the market? Have I drawn them in?
- Is there an obvious price action signal on the chart? e.g Pin Bar, Engulfing Patterns etc
- If there is an obvious signal, does it have confluence?
- What confluence does it have? Trend, Support / Resistance, 50% retrace level? The more the better…
- Is the signal showing rejection of a key market level?
- Is the signal showing a false-break of a key market level?

These are just some of the things you would want to look for as much as possible before you must regard such trade as a valid trade setup.

However, please note that whenever I am trading the last two signals DRPO and B&B, I always want to check if it is form with Pin Bar or Engulfing patterns. If I cannt see any of these with the direction trading signals I will regard it as not valid.

Always trade the last two signals in conjunction with the previous two. You can see in our previous examples where we had DRPO or B&B set up, there was either a Pin Bar, Inside Bar or Engulfing pattern to strengthen the trade set up. If you cannt see any of this, it will be better to avoid the trade. The market is always around and opportunities abound everywhere in the market. If you miss a trade today, you will surely get another perfect trade setup other time.

Let's do a recap-

Our Trading Signals are

- Pin Bars
- Grabber
- 2 Bar Reversals Pattern
- Engulfing Patterns
- DRPO
- B&B

They are only valid and tradable if they are formed on either Support or Resistance.

CHAPTER FIVE

WHEN A TRADE SETUP WILL FAIL

I will like to share with you in this chapter what to look for if a trade signal will not work or fail and how to avoid the not so perfect set up and opt for the ones that will move on time in the direction of trade.

- ✓ **Stalling Price After A Pin Bar**

Normally if you are trading Pin Bar or Engulfing Patterns, apart from the fact that they will sometime retrace to find a level of support to gather strength for the move in line with the direction of trade. Any time you are trading a Pin Bar and for the next 2 or 3 days, the price is not moving up or down rather making a side way movement, then it is best to get out of that trade. It might not work.

A Pin Bar that will work will move in your direction in the next day or two and you will see it on the chart, but once you see a trade stalling and stalling to move in your direction of trade. Get out of the trade and pay the spread.

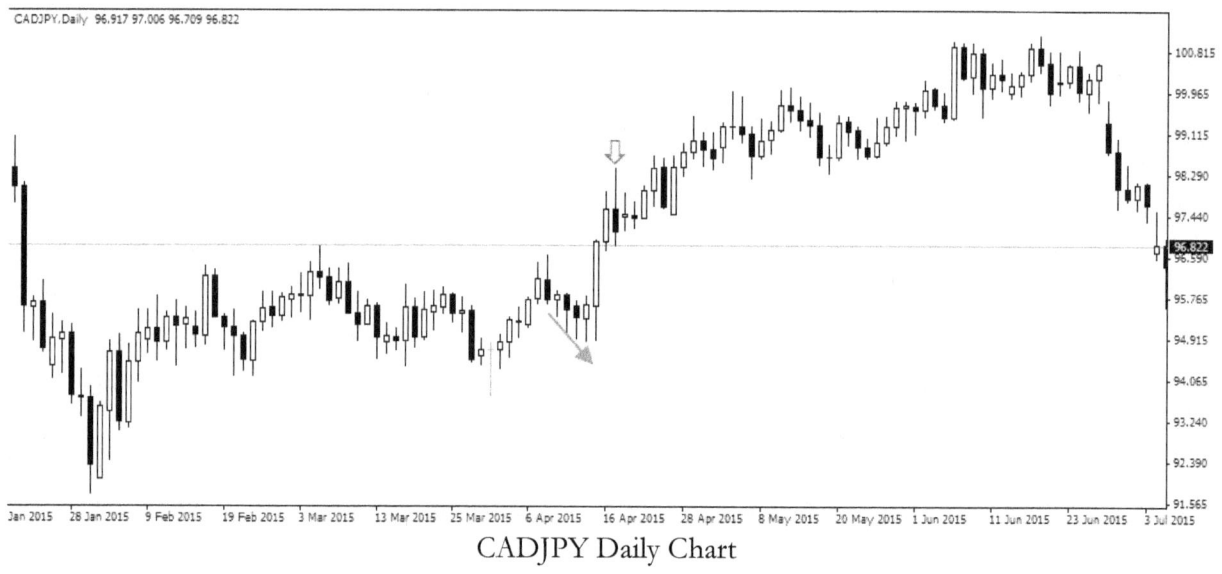

CADJPY Daily Chart

For instance in the above chart of CADJPY, you can see the bearish grabber pin bar indicated with the arrow. If you are in this trade and the price is not moving down as expected and is making a side way movement or stalling as seen in the next two days, then you should know the trade wont work, is better to get out and do not wait till price hit your stop loss thinking the trade might still work.

Look at the Pin Bar indicated by the Green Arrow, you will see that even though it wont reverse the end long enough, at least it make the market leave where it was to form a new low before it formed another in Bar to move the price up. That is one of the ways to know if a Pin Bar will work or not.

AUDNZD Daily Chart

This is another example of a stalling price action after a Pin Bar.

✓ **Using Stochastic To Determine Momentum**

I use stochastic as part of my trading arsenal alongside the trading signal. I used 5, 3, 3 as the settings for my stochastic. When the fast stochastic cross the slow stochastic from below up, it gives a buy signal and when it cross above down it gives a sell signal. That is the normal way to use it. But over time, I discover that stochastic can be used to determine the momentum in the market. When a price will move fast in a certain direction, you will know from the movement of the stochastic on the chart.

For instance, if you are using stochastic to determine when to buy or sell, assuming you want to buy and the fast stochastic has cross above the slow stochastic to the upside around 20 level and you place your trade- ay. Before the stochastic reach the 80 and above level, it might take 2 -3 days depending on the market momentum. But when the stochastic has touched or almost touched the opposite boundary in a day after the formation of the signal. That shows the momentum for that trade signal is exhausted, it is good and better to get out of the market before it goes against you.

For instance, let's look at the chart below

EURCAD Daily Chart

In this chart, the way and how fast the stochastic has moved towards the 20 level from above (80 levels) a day after the formation of the trade signal indicates that the momentum for the downside in this pair signal is getting exhausted.

Normally if the trade will move downward as expected, the crossing of the fast and slow stochastic line should still be around the 80 level, but when you see a fast movement downward or upward within one o two days after the signal, it is to tell you the momentum is exhausted, you might need to get out of the marke

You can see that this was also indicated by the price action on the chart. After the formation of the bearish Grabber on 13th July 2015, the next day (14th July 2015) price was still on the same level, instead of it to continue to sell as expected.

This is another example on EURUSD pair.

GBPUSD Daily Chart

In the GBPUSD chart above, the arrow shows a Pin Bar that was formed on 13th July 2015. When you check the stochastic you can see that it cross up while the candle is telling you to sell. Now this is to let you know that as far as the market is concern, the pin bar will best be regarded as a retracement or respect of resistance level (around 1.55898 – 1.56791) the momentum to the upside is still strong as shown by the movement of the stochastic. Apart from this, the candle was not formed at any key level. And you can see that the price rally up strongly and nullify the pin bar.

USDCAD Daily chart

In this USDCAD pair, I will show you why you should stay away from this type of set up. The Pin bar was formed around the Resistance level; there is no doubt about that. But if you look at the movement of the stochastic it has not cross above downward, it is still showing indication to move up. In this case, what it means is that, it might likely go up to test the resistance again before the Pin Bar can work. Will you like to enter a market that will go against you for some days before you eventually manage to scale through? I don't

want such a set up. I avoid it as much as possible. So also should you. I want to see a Pin Bar formation where the stochastic is indicating sell or buy by its movement around 80 or 20 level.
See our Ideal Trade Set Up Below

This is an ideal trade set up you should always look to trade. You can see the direction of the stochastic all the time the pin bar was formed. The first one indicated by the blue arrow, the pin bar is telling you to buy, and stochastic is saying the same thing by its cross above. The result you can see. Also the green arrow, candle and indicator align in the same direction.

The red arrow shows that the momentum to the upside will still continue provided you want to trade this pin bar. Any trade set up that you cannot get this type of conference, stay away from it.

USDPLN Chart- An Ideal Trade Set Up with Stochastic

FOREX MADE EASY

EURGBP Daily Chart- Ideal Trade Set Up

✓ **Don't Buy or Sell Into Key Levels**

Any trade you place very close to support or resistance might not work. A good way to trade is to place your trade around support or resistance and place your profit target in the next key level you see in the direction of you trade. But when you trade against key level your account is at risk for the trade might not work. It might go against you for sometime before it come back to retest the level. We don't want to place such a trade. This should be avoided at all cost.

EURUSD Daily Chart

This is an example of trading into key levels. Here the Support zone is mark by the horizontal line, to trade this kind of set up is risky. Why? No matter how strong and powerful the signal you are trading, market will always respect a key zone.

You can see that instead of the price to move down strongly the next day, it was held back by the support zone. Until the price breaks this support then we are sure the signal will work. If not, the best way to deal with this type of situation is

1. Stay away or
2. Wait till the market break the zone (break out) before you enter the market.

See another example here

EURCAD Daily Chart

The area of support is marked by the red horizontal line. The market is reacting to the support zone that was why it has not sold as expected. You will need a bearish break of this resistance turned support before you can trade this kind of set up. But is best to find a set up that wont be hinder by any obstacle until your target is reach.

Sample Ideal Trade Set Up

I have included here series of examples of how to trade one of the signals – Pin Bar and what to look for (evidences or conference) alongside.

In all of these trades, we are trading Pin Bar

Evidence One:

The Pin Bar was formed on Support or Resistance – you can see that on the chart.

Evidence Two:

Each time the Pin Bar indicated whether to buy or sell, the stochastic confirm what the signal is saying. This is an alignment between the candle and indicator. Evidence we must always look for.

Evidence Three:

Some of the Pin Bar was formed to reverse the trend, while some were formed to end a retracement.

The examples below were all taken from GBPCHF Daily Chart

FOREX MADE EASY

FOREX MADE EASY

CHAPTER SIX

RISK AND MONEY MANAGEMENT STRATEGY

Risk and money management is the act of managing your capital to trade in such a way that even if there are times of loses in your trading you are still in business. You can have a good strategy as I have shared with you in this book, if you don't have a good money management, you will soon blow your account or just breaking even, even if you do at all.

I must let you know that good money management with a trade plan is like the driver that will drives you to your destination in the Forex business. Lose it, and you are inviting your exit out of the business very soon.

RISK

After you have found a valid and tradable signal, the next thing you need to calculate is your risk. **How much am I risking in this trade? How much will I profit from this trade?** This should be the next agenda you need to sort out before you place your trade.

It is a common slogan in Forex business that don't risk more than 2-3% of your capital. While this philosophy is good, I believe how much you risk has to do with the personality of the trader. Assuming we have 5 different traders each with a capital of $1000. Some can conveniently lose $100 in all their trades combine without affecting their emotions, while some cannot afford that large loss. They are okay with $50 or less on $1000 capital.

In my own trading style, I am okay with 10% of my capital. That is my risk for any volume of trade I take. But don't risk more than 10% at most. You can start with 2-3% of your capital. Look at a percentage of your capital that when the trade goes against you, you wont bite your finger and get depressed. If 2% or 3% or 5% is okay with you stick with it. Find what works for you and stick with it.

For instance if am trading with $1000 capital. I am comfortable with $100 risk per trade. It may not be in one trade alone, assuming I am trading 2 pairs; I will have to use the position sizing to determine the lot size to trade in each trade so as not lose more than $100 in both trades assuming it goes against me. And if it is just one trade, the maximum am comfortable losing is $100.

The essence of staying with a comfortable risk – money management is to ensure you are in business even if you have series of losses consistently. Now assuming I have $1000 capital and my maximum risk is 3%. This means if I lose per trade, I am okay with $30. Now with 3% risk per trade, assuming I keep losing each trade. I will have to lose 33 times before I blown my capital. If I use 10% maximum risk, I will have to keep losing for up to 10 times consecutively before I blown $1000 account.

This understanding must be factor in when you are trading so that you don't just take any lot size whenever you want to trade. But the good news is that with a good trading strategy like the ones I shared with you in the previous chapters. It is impossible to lose consistently in a row except you are not doing the right thing.

If you are trading Pin Bar alone. (Back chart and count the number of times Pin Bar formed on the chart for a given time period). You will discover that even if it does not work, maybe at most 3 trades out of 10 trades. That means if you are risking $30 per trade. And your reward is $30. The total of 10 trades is $30 x 10 = $300 while your total loses is $30 x 3 = $90. Your profit at the end of your total trades will be $210. It could be more than this provided you are getting a reward of twice of your risk.

REWARD

Once you factor in your risk. The next thing to look for is your Reward. Reward is how much this trade will give me back in profit if it works. I am risking $30, will I be able to get up to $60 or more than what am risking? The most acceptable risk-reward ratio is 1:2.

That means find out if the trade will give you up to twice the amount you are risking. Sometimes you may not get up to that. Maybe 1:1 or 1:1.5 but is better if you can get at least 1:1.5 risk-reward ratio.

Let look at this scenario. I have a starting capital of $1000. My risk is 10% which is $100. In a month if the total number of trades I am able to trade is 10. The risk-reward ratio is 1:2 that means for every risk of $100, I get $200 back in profit.

Now out of 10 trades. I won 5 and lost 5 trades.
- successful trades will give me $200 x 5 = $1000 (For every successful trade with a risk of $100 I get $200 back in profit)
- Unsuccessful trades will give me $100 x 5 = $500

My total profitable trade is $1000, while my loss is $500. At the end of the month, I will have $500 profit added to my capital or equity.

Now imagine if the risk-reward ratio is 1:1. That means for each successful trade, I will get $100 back in profit for risking $100. With the same total number of loses and wins.
- successful trade will earn me $500 while,
- unsuccessful trades will earn me $500 as well.

At the end of the month, I will just break even. No profit no loss.

We are in Forex business to profit not to just break even. It is very necessary and vital to always look for a trade that will earn you much more than what you are risking per trade. This is why a good risk-reward ratio of 1:2 or 1:1.5 will still make you profit at the end of the month than just risking your money for every 1:1 risk-reward trade you see.

POSITION SIZING

After you have determined you risk and your reward the next thing is your position size. Position sizing comes in when you want to place you trade. Position sizing is the glue that holds risk to reward ratio together. **It helps you to know how many lot size will I place for this trade with this particular risk.**

For instance, if I am risking $30 in a trade, and the stop-loss is 100pips that means the trade will have to go against me 100 pips before I lose $30. Then on my broker's platform I will need to calculate a lot size that will give me a pip value that will amount to $30 for 100pips.

Depending on the type of account you open micro or standard account. Open a demo account and open trades in each lot size starting with 0.01lot to know the equivalent in pip for each currency you want to trade. One standard lot size is $10 per pip value. For some currency it may not be $10 may be $9.98 or less than that. You can use this formula (Divide your Risk Amount by your Stop Loss)

Now assuming you were able to calculate that 0.01lot size will gives you $0.1 pip value, 0.02 lot size will give you $0.2 pip value etc. Once you discover this, then with 100 stop loss, every 100pips will give you $10. To lose $30, then the appropriate lot size to trade will be 0.03.
This means a pip value will be equivalent to $0.3 ($30/100pips) and this trade will have to move against you for about 100pips before you lose $30 from that trade.

Your risk will determine the position size to use. It is not your stop loss. Most traders mess up in position sizing by fitting their stop loss to their desired position size instead of fitting their position size to their desired stop loss. For instance, if I am trading Gold and the set up gives requires a stop loss of 150pips, and my risk is $30. My Calculated reward is $60. The Lot size to take will be 0.02 lot size. For every $0.2 pip move, 150pips move will be equivalent to $30.

To illustrate the example of adjusting your position size to fit the necessary stop loss let's look at a daily chart of AUDNZD currency pair below.

Risk-Reward Ratio

Suppose our desired risk amount is $30, but our necessary stop loss distance is 87 pips, because the safest spot for our stop loss in this example is just below the low of the pin bar. So, after dividing the risk amount by the stop loss distance ($30 / 87), we get 0.345. Now, some brokers allow you to trade micro-lots, this basically means you have the flexibility to trade a position size as small as 1 penny per pip, in this case you would trade 3.4 micro lots (0.34 cents per pip), at 0.34 your risk will be just under $30 (0.34 x 87 = $30.0). If you use a broker that does not allow micro-lot trading then mini-lots are your next option, typically these are flexible up to .10 cent increments, this means you can trade .10 cents per pip at the smallest position size. In this case you would just trade .30 lots which would be (0.30 x 87) $26.1 risked. This is how you should view position sizing; always adjust the number of lots you trade (position size) to meet the stop loss distance that gives your trade the best chance of profiting.

NEVER adjust your stop loss to meet a desired position size, this is GREED.

Try as much as possible to know the pip value of each pairs you trade with respect to the kind of account you open to help you decide the choice of the appropriate lot size to trade.

Besides always **keep your risk consistent and never ever touch your trade while your trade is still live**. The setup is only invalided when your stop loss is hit or you trade a set up that stalls for the next 2 - 3 days. Assuming you are trading a pin bar, you will regard the pin bar trade to be invalid if price breaks the high or low of the Pin bar. It is normal for a Pin bar trade to retrace within the body of the pin bar. As long as the low or high is not broken, the trade is still valid and you will do yourself much favour if you don't touch the trade by exiting prematurely when it is going against you. This is why it is highly important to **do your analysis very well, calculate how much you are risking for that trade before you enter.** This will help you to wade off emotional sensations that may come in when the trade didn't move in your desired direction in time.

However, I must let you know that you need to Demo trade using capital that you would like to use for real trading i.e. you fund your demo account with $200 if you wish to start life trading with $200. Funding one's demo account with $5000 and you plan to start life trade with $200 won't make you well prepared for eventualities that such life trade would present. In other words, trade volume sentiments would not be well adjusted.

Another thing worthy of note is the fact that, small capital can easily be wiped off on higher time frame if **extreme cautions and money managements** are not well applied. You don't use 0.5 lot size on a 30mins chart with $200 or $500 capital and then switch to a daily chart with the plan to use the same lot size with the same capital! Adjust your position size with your risk.

NEVER RISK MORE THAN 5% AS A BEGINNER

CHAPTER SEVEN

TRADING AS A BUSINESS

Forex Trading is a business just as any business we have out there. There is a need to have a plan set aside that will guide you and hold you accountable on how you will implement your trading strategies and help you reach your target weekly or on a monthly basis. If you set up a physical business you will need to write your business plan. This also applies to trading. We call it Trading Plan.

Trading plan should be seen as a template or checklist for trading the market. This checklist will contain every aspect of your trading strategies together with risk and money management that acts as an objective guide to trade the market. It will also state your overall short and long term goals as a trader and provide you with a clear checklist of how to achieve them.

Success in the market is a function of discipline, and most people simply do not have enough self-discipline to determine if they are trading emotionally or objectively. This is the vacuum a trading plan is meant to fill. It will act as a guide which will keep you on the disciplined trading path. Once you have written your trading plan, you must ensure you hold yourself accountable to it. This is necessary for success in trading the market.

Most of us are accustomed to working a day job where you will resume work by 8am and leave by 5pm. This routine cycle of working hours hold us accountable to our boss. But in Forex, you are your own boss; you need something to hold you accountable so as avoid trading emotionally and pulling the trigger anytime we see the market move. Any trade set up we want to take must meet with every checklist on our trading plan or else is not worthy of risking our capital. Doing this will ensure we are trading objectively and not trading by emotions.

Trading plan helps you to;

- monitor your progress in Trading
- Hold yourself accountable and control the business

The following below are what you should include in your trading plan.

1. State your Short term and long term goals in trading the market
2. Date & Time to Trade
3. Define your trading strategies and all aspect of how you will analyze and trade the market
4. Define your money management strategy- this include your risk, reward
5. Currency pairs to trade

Let see an example of a typical trading plan

FOREX TRADING PLAN

Sample A

START-UP CAPITAL: $1000
TRADING GOALS
Short-Term Goals:
    To make consistent profits and supplement my monthly income.
    To be a discipline and profitable trader
Long-Term Goals:
    To build my account size up to $10000 through my trading strategy
TRADING STRATEGY
    Scan the Market for Pin Bar, Engulfing patterns, DRPO and B&B Trading Strategy on the Daily Chart
TIME TO ANALYZE: At the end of each market day
CRITERIA TO TRADE
    Pin Bar/Engulfing pattern formed on Key Levels with other supporting Evidence like Divergence, Position of Stochastic (Sell or Buy Signal)
CURRENCY PAIRS
    All Markets at least 20 pairs
RISK&MONEY MANAGEMENT
    Maximum Risk exposure per trade= 3% ($30)
    Reward: Minimum of twice my risk =6% ($60)
    Withdrawal Amount Per month = 10% of my current balance

Sample Plan B

Capital: $1000

Risk Per Volume of Trade: 3% ($30)

Time Frame: 4hrs, Daily

Target: $400 per week

Nos of Trade to Meet Target: minimum of 2 trades per week

Market: All Markets including commodities, 20 pairs

Strategy: Pin Bar, Engulfing Pattern, with DRPOs

Entry Criteria:

- ✓ Pin Bar/Engulfing on Key Zones
- ✓ Stochastic Position (Buy or Sell) in line with Pin Bar direction
- ✓ Divergence (Yes or No)

Exit Criteria:

Exit when profit target is hit.

A trading plan should be flexible and specific to you and your personality. You can also state you weekly Target and Monthly target and strategy you want to employ to achieve this. But a good trading plan must have an element of the above sample.

You need Discipline to implement your trading Plan. It is not enough to have a trading plan; you must ensure you follow your trade with your trading plan. This is the only way you will be successful and remain profitable over time in trading the market.

CHAPTER EIGHT

CONCLUSION

Apart from having a good strategy as I have shared with you above and the necessary prerequisites to trade successfully. It is paramount to have a good reliable and trustworthy broker to trade on their platform. When I started trading, I was introduced to one of the familiar broker out there. My experience with this broker was very bad. They hunt my stop and I had series of slippage on their platform which I called their attention to, unfortunately for me they use their terms and conditions to rob me of my money. Many other traders who use their platform also experience this same issue. I had to dump their platform and look for a better broker who will be plain and honest in transacting business with me.

If you want to know a good broker, the first thing you will do is to search for Reviews about their services from other traders who have been using their platform. You can search on Google or you go to forexpeacearmy.com under broker review, you will see a list of all the brokers and the views of several trader all over the world about their platform.

The second thing you look for is Customer Service. How fast do they reply when you mail them about an issue or problem you are facing on their platform? Customer Service Relations is a key integral part of any business. No matter how good your product is, if a business lacks good customer relations, is just a matter of time the company will fold up. Customers have a way of spreading good news about a company that treats them well likewise otherwise. Great customer service is a key. If you mail a broker and the broker takes 3-4 days to answer your query or they don't even reply you back at all, avoid such a broker.

The next thing you look for is their services. What do they offer? What instruments or currency can you trade on their platform? Do they have Bonus on deposits? And several stuffs like that. You must search on their website to find out what they offer and what makes them better than others.

These are some of the few brokers I used to trade. Since I have been trading with them I don't have any issue. So I can recommend them to you.

InstaForex

InstaForex is an ECN-broker operating on the Forex exchange market since 2007. Over 2 million traders have become the company's customers around the world. More than 1,000 clients open new trading accounts every day. InstaForex clients have access to a wide number of opportunities for effective and profitable trading on Forex. Their 24/7 technical and customer support is always at your fingertips. Even traders who invest small amounts are able to get big profit.

They offer program products such as the PAMM system under which one can invest in the most successful traders. Another option is ForexCopy– a trade copy service – which gives you the chance to duplicate the success of more experienced traders, thus gaining on Forex without much effort.

This is one of the Bonus offer by Instaforex

250 % Deposit Bonus

It is a beneficial offer for new clients who have not registered accounts with InstaForex yet.

Open an account with instaforex and get 250% on your deposit.

No Deposit $30 Deposit

Earning on the forex market without depositing money is absolutely real. InstaForex gives every new client a remarkable opportunity to get a start-up capital. So, you will be able to set to trading without investing your money.

The No Deposit Bonus can be withdrawn after executing buy or sell deals of the total volume equal to X*25 InstaForex lots in total where X is the total amount of the bonuses received (all the bonuses ever gained are taken into account, including cancelled or partially lost ones). Only the whole bonus amount is allowed for withdrawal, there is no possibility to partially withdraw the bonus. In order to withdraw bonus funds from your trading account, please send your request to bonuses@instaforex.com. The bonus to be withdrawn must be on your account at the moment when your request is being considered. The company reserves the right to reject the withdrawal request without giving any explanations. The profit derived from the No Deposit Bonus is allowed for withdrawal only in case it exceeds 20% of the bonus amount. Profit of any kind exceeding 20% is available for withdrawal.

PAMM Account

InstaForex system of PAMM accounts is a reliable way to invest funds in other traders' deals with no restrictions. Every user of the PAMM system can make a profit free of risk by attracting investors. You can invest with as low as $1

Check the monitoring account of traders on their website.

Instaforex has a very good customer service. They reply your query very fast like the speed of light. I mailed them about 7:12am and less than 3hrs time I got a reply (9:53am). See a snapshot below. This is what you look for in a good broker.

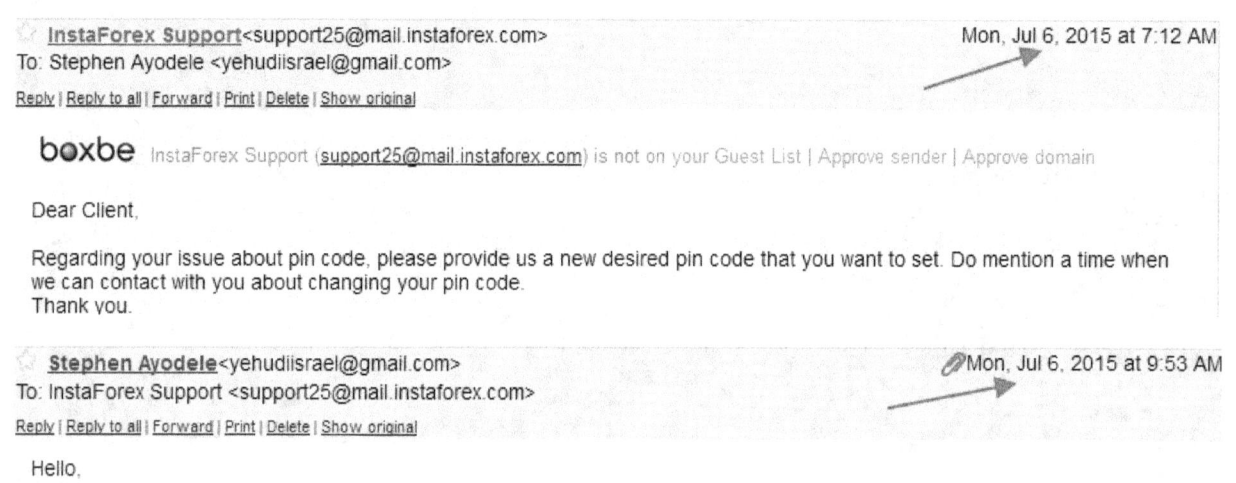

Unfortunately, **they do not accept USA citizen as a client**. Every other country citizen can apply.

XM Broker

www.xm.com

With over 300,000 Real Accounts opened since it was founded in 2009, XM has grown to a large and well established international investment firm and has become a true industry leader. XM is headquartered in Cyprus with representative offices operated in the strategic locations of Hungary and Greece.

XM currently employs more than 150 professionals whose combined expertise represents the greatest talent pool to be found at any forex broker. Their extensive experience combined with support for well over 20 languages, makes XM the broker of choice for traders of all levels, anywhere. They have the expertise and the resources to help everybody realize their investment goals, like only a big broker can.

- Over 300,000 accounts opened
- Traders from 196 countries
- 25 secure payment methods
- 8 full feature trading platforms
- More than 20 languages supported
- 24/5 personal customer service
- Trading with XM means trading with a broker who is fair and reputable. XM is licensed and regulated by CySEC and ASIC.
- All clients enjoy the same fair and ethical trading conditions regardless of their net capital worth, the size of their investment, or their account type.

Why Choose XM?

- XM fosters a sustainable workforce development through a wide spectrum of cultures, and approaches your needs with openness to cultural, national, ethnic and religious diversity. Their advanced trading platforms and flexible trading conditions suit a diverse global clientele. Their expertise is derived from extensive experience and in-depth knowledge of the global financial markets. They are dedicated to delivering superior services in currency trading, along with CFDs, equity indices, precious metals, and energies.
- The operational philosophy they follow is simple: by ensuring client satisfaction, they earn their loyalty. "Our reputation is linked to our credibility, both of which stem from our ability to service our clients in the way that they expect and deserve. We have never made any compromises in factors that can affect client performance, which is why we offer tight spreads and the best execution available anywhere."
- Trade Forex with No Requotes. Experience XM Legendary Execution.
  You can gain Access to 8 Trading Platforms from 1 Account.

50% bonus is automatically added to any deposits made in your account up to $500 or currency equivalent. Every funded client has the opportunity to automatically enroll in the XM loyalty program which rewards them XMP (XM Points) on every trade they make, allowing them to earn endless rewards.

And there is Zero fees on Deposits and Withdrawals

Please note that XM do not accept clients from New Zealand, USA, Quebec Canada. They accept from UK and Brazil etc.

XTM - Forex Broker

ForexTime (FXTM) is an international online forex broker. The company is the brainchild of Andrey Dashin, a renowned businessman known for his business insight and entrepreneurial mind.

The company is regulated by the International Financial Services Commission of Belize.
Our aim is to offer the best possible services to our clients, who are our prime priority and to whom we are extremely dedicated.

- Regulated by IFSC under license numbers IFSC/60/345/TS and IFSC/60/345/APM
- Trading services in FX, spot metals & various CFDs
- Multilingual customer support team & representative offices across the globe
- Free educational courses/webinars for all client

FXTM offers Rebates for trading. They offer you the chance to be able to get back your money when you place a trade. Highest rebates of 25% of Spread & Commissions. If you have a live account, go to your client Cabinet and click on Zero cost promotion.

This is one of the ways I trade with FXTM and gets back money even if the trade is a losing trade. You can click on the link below to open an FXTM account if you have not.

www.forextime.com

Forextime Ltd does not offer its services to residents of certain jurisdictions such as the USA, Japan, British Columbia, Quebec, Saskatchewan and Iran.

These are the four brokers I use for my trading. One of the benefit of using many brokers is that if on broker A the candlestick chart for a particular signal I want to trade is not displaying very well due to time zone difference, if I check broker B I will see it clearly and still place the trade

Finally start with Pin Bar first, once you have develop your confidence and master this trading strategy you can add 2 Bar Reversal Pattern, Engulfing patterns and DRPOs' with it in that order.

Demo trade for some time and when you switch to a live account make sure you strictly adhere to a good money management principle of not trading more than 5% of your account per time. If you don't do this, despite the good strategy in your hand, you will still find it very hard to make a living from the Forex Market.

I strongly believe if you implement this strategy you will get an edge over the market and trade profitably

If you have any enquiries, feedback and any issues in your trading kindly contact me through the address below. I am going to reply and put you through in your trading journey.

Best of luck in your Trading.

Stephen Benjamin

Mail: microejobs@gmail.com